THE DEATH OF A CHILD

A BOOK FOR FAMILIES

TESSA WILKINSON was, until recently, a bereavement counsellor for the Helen House children's hospice in Oxford. It was during the course of her work that she realised the need for a book about the death of a child which spoke to both parents and children alike. Tessa Wilkinson is married with two teenage sons.

THE DEATH OF A CHILD

A BOOK FOR FAMILIES

Tessa Wilkinson

Illustrated by Gavin Rowe

WITH A FOREWORD BY
SISTER FRANCES DOMINICA
OF HELEN HOUSE

Julia MacRae Books

LONDON SYDNEY AUCKLAND JOHANNESBURG

Part of the proceeds from the sale of this book will be donated to the work of Helen House.

First published in Great Britain 1991
by Julia MacRae
an imprint of Random House
20 Vauxhall Bridge Road, London SW1V 2SA
Random House Australia (Pty) Ltd
20 Alfred Street, Milsons Point, Sydney, NSW 2061
Random House New Zealand Ltd
18 Poland Road Glenfield, Auckland 10, New Zealand
Random House South Africa (Pty) Ltd
PO Box 337, Bergvlei, 2012, South Africa

Reprinted 1991, 1993

Designed by Douglas Martin
Typeset in Perpetua by Tek Art Ltd, Addiscombe, Croydon, Surrey
Printed and bound in Great Britain by Butler & Tanner Ltd, Frome, Somerset

British Library Cataloguing in Publication Data is available
ISBN 1-85681-250-2

CONTENTS

To DAVID ARCHER, HENRY CARPENTER *and* URSULA DOWNING

Through their deaths I began to understand life

THANKS *to all the families at* HELEN HOUSE *who let me come and walk beside them for a while, and who taught me so much; to my husband* GUY *without whom I would never have managed to write this book, and to* PETER HUNT *who encouraged and helped me so much.*

FOREWORD BY

SISTER FRANCES DOMINICA
OF HELEN HOUSE

In a culture where we have come to see longevity as our right, the death of a child is experienced as outrageous. The family will be grief-stricken, but the ripple-effect will extend far beyond the immediate relatives. For the most part even more distant friends and acquaintances are ill-prepared to cope with their own reactions, let alone those of the people closest to the child. Embarrassment or fear of saying the wrong thing frequently mean that people instinctively step aside, hoping fervently that there are "experts" around to support those who grieve most deeply. The resulting loneliness for the family is very hard to bear. Just when you need your friends most they seem not to be around.

By her sensitive but straight-forward approach in this book I believe Tessa Wilkinson will help those who read it to believe that they themselves are experts, for we are well equipped with a shared humanity, and all the frailty and the nobility that that implies. Tessa has offered friendship to many people who are grieving. She has listened more often than she has talked and so now she is able to offer her readers an approach which combines practical common sense and compassion with the wisdom and understanding of a dedicated student who has sat at the feet of the greatest experts, those who have themselves experienced the tragic death of a beloved child.

If *The Death of a Child* brings a little comfort, directly or indirectly, to those who grieve I know that the author will have achieved what she set out to do.

INTRODUCTION

Fourteen years ago I had a telephone call at home from a dear friend. She rang to say would I come quickly, her son had died. He was just ten weeks old. She had gone to get him out of his carry-cot, and had found him dead. Before this, the closest I had ever been to death was the death of my grandparents when I was a child, but I was not very much involved emotionally and had not attended their funerals. Suddenly I was made to face death directly, the death of a ten-week-old child.

I went to my friend; I have no idea what I said or how I coped with her emotions and my own. But somehow we survived that day together, and the following very dark weeks and months that she and her husband went through.

The next time that I had to confront death was once again the death of a child who was attending the nursery school I was running. I knew that she was very ill, and could die at any time. Nevertheless, when I received a call from her mother one morning to tell me that she had died during the night, it still came as a tremendous shock. She had always pulled through her other crises, and somehow I assumed that she always would. Again, I spent time with her parents during the hours following her death. I saw her body lying in her parents' bed. I had never seen a dead body before and I went with great apprehension. In fact, seeing her body removed all the fear that I had; she looked peaceful and out of pain, and somehow empty as if the vital part of her was missing. I found that very comforting.

Some years afterwards I went to live in Oxford, and in 1982 I started to work at Helen House, a children's hospice. The idea behind the foundation of Helen House was to have a place where children who were chronically sick with a life-threatening illness could come for respite or terminal care. It was the first children's hospice in the world; I was privileged to be there when it opened its doors for the first time. It is a small unit with just eight beds, very much a home from home. It offers families a place to bring their children when they need some rest from looking after them. They can either stay with their children, or leave them and go home, or take a holiday. The aim of Helen House is to help these families to keep their children at home, recognising that looking after a sick child for any length of time, whether it be for weeks, months or years, can be exhausting, and that some back-up support is needed. It is not sophisticated, as a hospital would be; it does not offer medical intervention. Its main aim is to be a home from home, offering love, care and support for all the family – parents, grandparents, brothers and sisters. The children who come to Helen House can be any age up to sixteen. How often they come and for how long will vary from family to family. Some will come fairly frequently, others will perhaps come once a year while the family take a holiday. The important thing is that the family know Helen House is there when they need help, 24 hours a day, 365 days a year. Although all the children who come to Helen House will die from their illness, it is primarily a place to live, full of light and laughter.

Working at Helen House, I was meeting once again the death of children. The experience of past years had made me reflect a little on death, particularly the unexpected death of a child. Now I was to meet families every day who were facing the prospect of their child dying.

From the start the team at Helen House heard the same thing from the families who came to us: how hard it is that people do not seem to know how to cope with a very ill child; in particular we heard how isolated and alone families felt after a child had died. Parents told us the all-too-familiar story of people crossing the road to avoid the awkwardness of not knowing how to greet them before and after the bereavement. But what can anyone say to a mother whose child has just been diagnosed as suffering from a life-threatening illness? What can be said when a colleague returns to work after his child's funeral? What does a teacher say to a pupil whose sister has died? What does a school do if a child who attends the school has died? How can grandparents be confronted after they have been to their grandchild's burial? So many difficult encounters, all of which people would probably prefer to avoid. I hope this book will help families and friends who find themselves in such situations to understand their feelings a little better.

During the first three and a half years at Helen House we cared for fifty families whose children had died, and many more whose children would die in the months and years to come. Experience led us to believe that it would be good to have a specific person to work with the bereaved families. The need seemed to be for someone to visit, and to *keep* visiting, the families during the dark months or years following the death of their child. We felt that it might help to offset the isolation so many of the families were feeling. I agreed to take on that job and have been working as a bereavement visitor now for four years.

In the course of my work I have become increasingly aware of the need for a simple book to help both adults and children. This book arose from that need. The book is in two sections: the first section looks at the death of a child and the following bereavement in some detail. It is written for adults, to help them gain some insight into coping with a child's death. The second part is written for children, to be used with adults. It is a short simple story with pictures, about the death of a child as seen through the eyes of another child. If a child dies, other children are affected;

not just those in the family, but friends from school or clubs or the neighbourhood. It is important that these other children have the opportunity to understand a little bit about what has happened and try to make death a less uncomfortable part of life. Finally, at the end of the book I have included some poems and readings that families have found helpful and have used at funeral services, together with a list of organisations who help the bereaved.

As Helen House's bereavement visitor, I have learned so much from families who have had to cope with the death of a child. It is this knowledge that I want to share with a wider audience. I hope that it will help anyone who has to face the death of a child: the bereaved families themselves; the 'professionals' – the nurses, doctors, health visitors, social workers, teachers and clergy – and those who just meet death in their everyday life as I did. Death is part of everyone's life, and we never know when we shall meet it.

PART ONE

As I travel around the country visiting families whose children have died, one thing is said to me again and again: "If only people stopped for a moment and tried to think what it would be like if a child they loved was to die. If they did, I am sure they would begin to understand how we feel." I hear many stories of the bereaved feeling isolated and abandoned by family and friends. I hear stories of people saying things without thinking first. I hear stories of people saying nothing at all, just avoiding, and walking away. The picture I get is one of the ordinary person in the street and even the professional not knowing what to do or to say when they come face to face with a grieving family.

Death is not a subject which is talked about openly, and yet it is the one thing which is guaranteed to happen to all of us. Unless we allow death to become part of life, the taboo will never go away. Only a few decades ago many families would have known the death of a child. Every community had someone who laid out the body, usually in the family home. The coffin was made by the local carpenter, and kept in the house before the funeral. People dressed in black, and it was recognised that they were in mourning. Now most of that has gone. Today when someone dies, the undertaker is called to the house to remove the body as soon as possible. The washing of the body and the laying out is done by strangers in a strange place. The body is "viewed" in the Chapel of Rest, where it is not easy to touch or handle. We do not dwell on death, we tidy it away, and we pay others to deal with it for us. Because of this, it has become a frightening, unspoken subject.

It is therefore not surprising that many people do not know what to do or to say when they encounter it.

In this book I shall focus particularly on death caused by illness. Children's deaths may, of course, happen for many reasons: accidents, still birth, cot death, murder, suicide. Each type of death will bring its own problems to be faced and coped with. For example, if a child dies suddenly, whatever the cause, the police may have to be involved, which can mean extra distress; there will have been no time to prepare for the death, so shock will often be a part of the reaction; there may well be many questions needing answers, and those endless "if onlys" – "If only we had not let her go alone", "If only we had gone to her when she cried", "If only I had gone to the doctor sooner". With these "if onlys", there may well be feelings of guilt and soul searching. Blame may be laid on the other partner, or on other people perceived as having caused the death. There may be strong feelings of anger. Although I shall not be looking in detail at causes of death other than illness, what I shall say, especially about the grief felt after the death, may well apply to any family which has suffered the loss of a child.

Sometimes I am asked: "Isn't it easier for a family to cope with the death of their child if the child has been ill for some time, and the parents have been able to prepare themselves?" It seems to me impossible to give a simple answer to such a question. Is it "better" to see your child suffer for years from a long drawn out illness, and then die? Or is it "better" if they die suddenly? All that can be said is that however a child dies, it will be very hard to bear, for all the family and friends.

There is a widely held belief that it is necessary to be an expert in order to help bereaved people, that it is essential to be a trained counsellor, a professional. Nothing could be further from the truth. Grieving in itself is not an illness (although it may produce physical reactions); it is a natural part of bereavement, and bereavement is a natural part of life. It is a readjusting to a new situation, a moving on and a letting go. It can take several years to work through the journey of grief, and during that time families may suffer from very dark days. People can so easily help the bereaved through the dark days by being prepared to befriend them. You don't need to be trained to do this, just to come with an open, loving heart. Being open, loving, and *available*, not just in the first few weeks but for months and years – that is the best help that can be given.

Bereavement can start long before a child dies. From the moment that a child is diagnosed as having a life-threatening illness, the process of grieving will begin. That is not to say that the family gives up on the child and loses all hope, but deep down there may be a fear of what is to come, and a grief for what will never be. When a child is born it is normal for us to take for granted that there is a long life ahead. We assume that the grandparents and parents will die before the child. If these natural assumptions are challenged by a child's life-threatening illness, the shock is a painful one.

Some families are able to talk about their sadness, and share together their feelings of anxiety about what is to come. Others may be unable to share in such a way, and then problems can arise between husband and wife, or parents and children. If one person denies the inevitability of the death and the other one is wanting to talk about it, big stresses may occur. Sadly many marriages break up in such circumstances. The stress on a family looking after a sick child over a period of months or years can be enormous. There may be endless broken nights. Wives may feel neglected by husbands who continue to work, and so seem to have a break from the home situation. Husbands may feel neglected by their wives, who need to give so much of their time and energy to the sick child. Other children in the family may grow to resent the attention to the sick child, or may become jealous.

There are also difficult decisions to be made about authorising certain treatments, especially if the treatment is held out as being the only hope. Parents will have to face up to deciding whether or not it is right to put their child through unpleasant treatment or an operation: for example, the insertion of a tube for breathing directly into the throat (tracheotomy) may be used to prolong a life without touching the basic illness; radiotherapy and chemotherapy can have very unpleasant side-effects; bone marrow transplants may require long searches for appropriate donors and the ever-present risk of rejection. When there is no knowing beforehand what the outcome will be, or how much pain and discomfort the child may have to go through, such decisions are profoundly difficult. And it is also important that parents are reassured by the professionals with whom they are dealing, so that they do not come to feel that their children have been used as "guinea pigs" to further medical research – a situation which can arise if new techniques are being used without sufficient explanation.

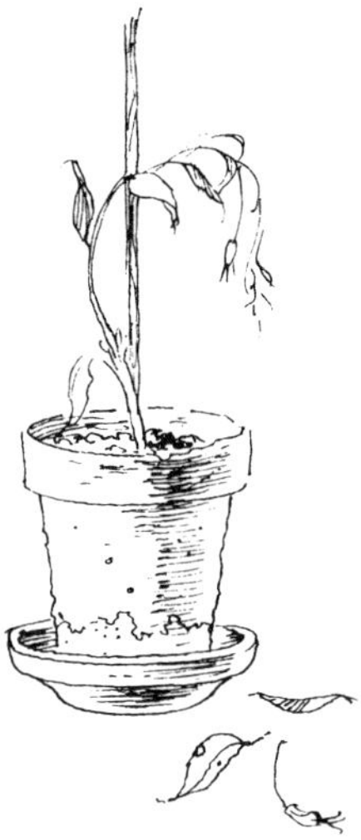

For some parents the acceptance of death as a natural ending allows them to feel that it is not absolutely necessary to try every means of keeping their child alive for a little longer; for others it is important for them to be able to feel that they have done everything medically possible for their child. There is no "right" way. Parents may find it very difficult to resist pressure put on them by doctors to try yet another form of treatment. Such pressures can arise if the doctors themselves find it hard to accept that death is an inevitable outcome, and not the result of their failure. It is fair to say that doctors, too, may need to learn to face death without feelings of guilt, especially where children are involved.

If there are other children in the family, it is important that their schools are kept informed about what is going on at home. It can be hard to be in a family with a child who is very ill. Children are often unthinkingly cruel to each other, especially if someone is "different". A child may be teased about his sick sister: "Your sister's got a funny face", "Your sister's going to die". It is important to watch out for these situations, so that help can be given where it is needed.

The routine of a family may be shattered because of hospital visits or unexpected remissions when the sick child comes home and seems almost "normal". It is hard for a family to plan anything ahead because plans so often must be changed. Family life can be very fragile. There may well be feelings of wanting the death to happen just to bring relief from the situation; but then guilt may follow – how can anyone "want" their child to die? Such feelings are very common, and it is important for all members of the family to recognise them, and not feel guilty.

One of the many difficult decisions which will have to be faced by parents is whether or not to talk to the child about his or her approaching death. There are no hard and fast rules. Some families will be able to talk very openly about dying and death, allowing it to become an open and accepted part of life. One sick child asked his mother as they were driving along in the car: "Mum, if I die before you, will your coffin go on top of mine?" Without a second thought his mother answered his question. She said that she liked the idea of them being buried together. They would have to make plans to acquire a double grave, she said, and of course, if her son died first, her coffin would then go on top of his. They could have their names engraved on the same headstone. For them, death had become a natural part of their life. Other families find such an open approach too painful, and so the subject is never shared. Indeed, games of protection may arise, when the parents say they cannot speak to the child, because it would be too upsetting for him, but the child may say he cannot talk to his parents because they always become so distressed when he tries to. If this happens, an outsider may be able to help the parents and their child to come together and talk openly about the child's death. It is essential that families should be encouraged to find the way most appropriate to them and, if possible, find they can talk openly amongst themselves. Though I stress again that there are no "rules", experience has shown that in the majority of cases families who can be persuaded openly to share their emotions and feelings find it easier to cope than those who bottle things up.

When the time of death is approaching, a family may need some gentle outside assistance; if a child is to die at home it can be helpful to have the support of a general practitioner, district nurse, or specialist nurse. Some families may need help with pain control, others may require special equipment, which should be readily available when needed. Sadly this is not always the case, and it greatly adds to the distress of the parents if they experience bureaucratic or other difficulties when they seek special equipment for their child.

It is important that the family does not have just one "special" person to help them through this time of death. If it can be arranged, several "special" people – a family doctor, a nurse, a close friend, a clergyman, etc. – should share together the possibility of being called to help. It is a big burden to be carried alone; several people helping can take it in turns to be on call while others have the opportunity to recharge their batteries. These people should not take over, but simply be available if needed. Some families just need to be told that what they are doing is all right, for at a time of such stress the need for loving reassurance is obviously great.

All through this time of dying, and during the few days after the death, the family should be allowed to "do" the death in their own way.

If a child and his family prefer the death to happen at home, and feel that they can cope, every support should be given to make this possible. If there is a fear of *not* coping, then the whole of this time may be handled more comfortably in hospital or in a hospice, particularly if it is a place that has already built up a good relationship with the family. Many families will seek hospital help when a crisis occurs, and want active medical treatment to continue in the hope of prolonging their child's life. If, however, a family chooses a hospice, they will know that active treatment to prolong life is not the priority. The priority of a hospice is to make the best of the life that remains to the child. Pain control and basic nursing care will be offered. The important thing is that the family makes up its own mind where to go, without pressure from others. Usually parents will have decided what sort of place they want to turn to when a crisis occurs, and will have had the opportunity to discuss it with their doctor. The medical profession should be aware of, and sensitive to, the parents' wishes and needs at this stage.

Some families will start thinking about and planning for this time long before it happens. They will consider whether to have a burial or cremation; where to hold the service; what sort of service to have. They may start thinking and talking about hymns, prayers and readings. Other families may feel that even thinking about such things is premature, almost as if they had given up, and so they make no plans at all until the death has happened.

Those who are involved in helping families sometimes become concerned if it appears that parents are not facing up to the fact that their child is dying. But this is not always apparent to outsiders and there are many not-so-devious ways of coping. One father talked at length about the summer holiday he and his family were going to take together when his daughter was better. They all knew in their hearts that it was unlikely to happen, but dreaming dreams was an important way for that father to cope. He was not, in fact, denying his daughter's approaching death, because a few moments later he would talk about it. It was as if he found it too painful to dwell on the death all the time. He needed his dreams, a seeming unreality which cloaked reality.

Another family stopped coming to see their tiny baby daughter because they felt that they had said their goodbyes. They feared that they might grow to love her too much; by not being with her all the time they hoped to protect themselves from too much pain when she died. To an outsider, this might seem hard, but for that family it was *right*. We cannot be judgemental.

The "professionals" should try to avoid telling any family how they should be feeling or coping. One mother was told by her health visitor that she should stop fighting for her son. Because he was dying she should start to let go. But that mother had to live on after her child had died, and she had to live with herself. If she felt that she had given up on the child, before he died, how might

she feel after his death? She needed to feel that she had done all she could for her son and it was important for her to follow her instincts in this respect. A professional can offer sympathy, practical help and advice, but cannot tell any family exactly what is *right* to do and what is *wrong*.

Because people facing the death of others may well feel vulnerable and frightened, it is particularly important that those who try to help them devote time to thinking about death, and what it means to each of them. We need to think about our own death, and about the death of those whom we love. If we have not taken time to think about such things, we may find it hard to help those who must think about them. To suggest to a mother that she should start "letting go" of her child, requires that we have some idea how we would feel if that same suggestion were to be made to us.

Helpers involved with grieving families must be careful that their own fears are not projected onto someone else. Unless we ourselves have started to face up to some of the ultimate questions that death poses it is unlikely that we shall have much to share with those who are living through the death of a child.

Two of the big questions parents often ask are: "What will happen when she dies?" or "How will she die?" There is no one answer to these questions. Usually doctors have some idea in advance as to the final physical cause of death, because this will to some extent depend upon the nature of the illness. Often doctors will warn parents of the worst conditions that might occur, such as haemorrhaging or continuous fitting, so that the family can begin to prepare themselves. In the event, however, the death is very often peaceful, which is what everyone hopes for. With many children, it becomes obvious that their condition is deteriorating and that they are dying. Their colour will change and their breathing will become very irregular. Gradually the gaps between each breath may become longer, and gently and quietly their breathing will stop. Television images of dramatic last gasps are seldom seen in reality. It is more usual for the child to slip gently away. There is much to be said for the parents being with their child at this time, if only just to hold his or her hand.

Many families speak of the moment of death as being something timeless, as if time stands still for a moment. They will speak of having a strong sense that their child's spirit has left the body, and of the body quite suddenly seeming empty. It is as if the essence of their child has gone, and only a shell is left behind. The idea of the body being like a chrysalis after the butterfly has flown free may be a helpful image. If the child has been severely disabled, the idea of a butterfly flying free can be a very beautiful one.

What should happen in those few hours after a child has died? There are many answers to that question. Perhaps ideally the answer should be: "What ever the family wants". But that is not always possible, because what happens will depend on where the death occurs, whether at home, in a hospice or in a hospital.

It can be important to ensure that at the time of death families are able to feel that they have plenty of time. There is really no need to hurry; if a family wants to spend time with the body, then that time should be found. Often it seems that everyone is in a great hurry to get the body out of the house, or out of the ward. There is a rush to tidy it up, to get it out of the way. But many people will say later that this time spent with their child's body was of great importance. Time to touch it, to hold it, to see it changing, to sense the emptiness. All these things can help the reality and the finality of death to sink in. A mother may wish to carry her dead baby into the garden. A father might want to hold his son's body for hours. An hysterical teenager may want to be alone with her brother's body. A mother may wail openly and noisily. A young child may keep going back to see his brother's body time and time again. There should be understanding of, and time for, these reactions.

This can be a time of uncertainty for those people – friends, relatives, other helpers – who are present and trying to help. They may feel a need to try to control what is happening. If the body is tidied away quickly, then the need to cope with these difficulties is reduced. Yet why should a mother not carry her child's body into the garden? It will certainly not harm the body, and it could make a big difference to the mother. The hysterical teenager needed to say goodbye to her brother in her own way and in her own time. Who is to say it was wrong? Of course the father should be able to hold his son's body for as long as he wants. Once those last precious hours are gone, he will never be able to hold his son again.

In the period immediately after death, some professional help may be needed with the next stage – the preparation of the body. However, that help should still enable the family to be in control of the situation. This may be a time when, however difficult it may be for others involved, there must be readiness to take risks with the bereaved family.

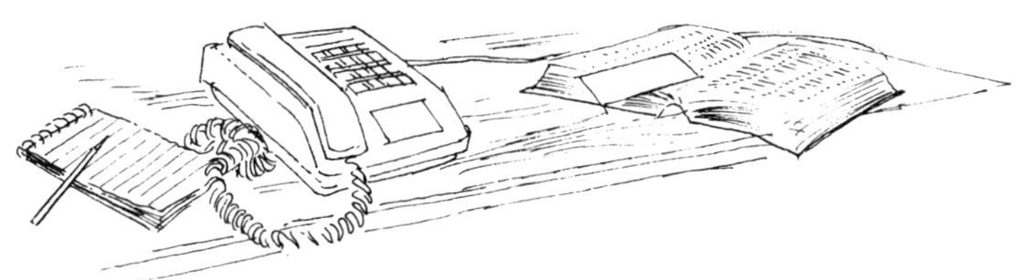

Families should be asked if they want the task of washing and dressing the body of their child. They may need to be told that it is up to them to "do" what they want, and if possibilities are gently suggested to them, it may provide them with the chance to decide how they want to cope. These things need to be suggested, because in the circumstances the family may be afraid to ask for fear that it is the "wrong" thing to do. If the assumption is that it is the undertaker or nurse who should wash the body, it may be very hard for the family even to express their own wishes. Again it is important that the "professionals" do not take over, without allowing the family every opportunity to be involved.

Many families will have chosen a special outfit for their child to wear in the coffin. Some like a pretty dress, others a favourite track suit, others still, football colours. One child wore a Spiderman outfit. It can be very important to the family to make the body look as "pretty" or "smart", as possible, and this should be absolutely their decision.

Sometimes undertakers put make-up on children and their families, unprepared, have found this very distressing. One mother said: "My son never wore make-up. I wanted to wash it off, but didn't like to." If a body has been badly damaged, make-up can be a big help in disguising the disfigurement, but make-up put on to disguise death is not helpful. Death is death, and painting rosy cheeks onto a dead child's face cannot hide that fact.

Once the body has been "laid out" the family might like to choose a favourite toy to go in the coffin, or to cut a piece of hair as a keepsake. Often brothers and sisters like to write little notes to go in the coffin. Flowers can be laid round the body. Some families like to take photographs. Again there is no hurry, and to go back to be with the body time and time again may be a help to a family, not least to brothers and sisters or other children. Often the reality of death is much gentler than an imagination left to roam. One brother said that he did not want to see his sister's body. When asked why not, he said: "When you die, your skin falls off and you become a skeleton." Children often have very frightening images of death given to them by television and video. Being involved and seeing the body may help to remove those fears, and it can be a reassuring experience for a child, rather than a distressing one.

Children often ask what happens when you die. Vague generalisations like: “She has gone to be with Jesus”, or “She is in heaven” are often given in reply. However it should be borne in mind that children may be confused if, having seen the body in the coffin, they are then told that their brother or sister has gone to heaven. When children ask very down-to-earth questions, it is important to give them honest and straightforward answers wherever possible. For example, to say: “He has fallen asleep” or “God wanted him more than we did” or, even more equivocally, “He’s gone on a long holiday”, may lead to problems and traumas in the future. Saying: “He has fallen asleep” may lead to a fear of going to sleep from which there is no waking up. Whatever expression is used, or whatever explanation is given, it should be one which parents can afterwards feel able to support or develop, because it is rooted in their beliefs or their understanding of death.

Care should be taken that other children in a family are remembered at this time, especially if the parents are very wrapped up in their own grief; after all, the rest of the family are bereaved as well, and have lost a brother or sister. They may need someone special who can keep an eye on them and explain what is happening. They may feel very frightened, since to see a parent crying, possibly for the first time, can in itself be deeply disturbing to a child, quite apart from the impact of the death of a brother or sister.

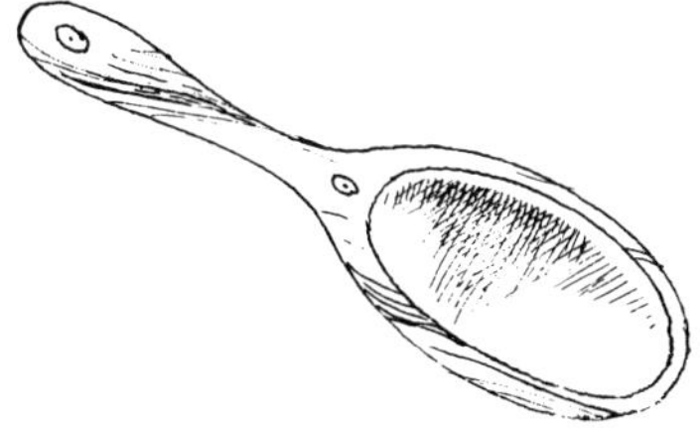

Children may need to be convinced that their brother or sister is really dead. They may be shown how to try to feel for the pulse or to hold a mirror up to the dead child’s mouth and to see how it does not mist up. They may be encouraged to feel the body and to discover how cold it is. They should also be told what will happen in the next few days. An explanation may be given about having to register the death, and they could be involved in arranging the funeral, perhaps by choosing a hymn or a piece of music. Someone should take time to explain what happens at a funeral or cremation. One child thought his brother's body would be taken out of the coffin when he was buried, and was very relieved when this did not happen. Children have powerful imaginations and this is a time when it is vitally important to treat them with respect, not to fudge the issue.

How soon the funeral should happen is up to the family, taking into account the availability of the church or crematorium and of the person who will lead the service. Some families feel that they want to get it over and done with as soon as possible; others want time to get things organised, and to give families and friends the opportunity to come.

Planning the funeral service can be a big problem for some families, especially if they have never been inside a church. It may be helpful if there is a collection of appropriate prayers and hymns available to show to the family. (There is a suggested list of prayers and readings which we have used at Helen House at the back of this book.) Families may wish to take any available suggestions away for a while, to look at in the quiet and safety of their home. If the child had a favourite piece of music, it can be played on a tape during the service. Again, it is important to stress that the family should have the service that they want. The funeral can be in the context of a religious service, or not. If the family have no particular religious faith, it should be possible to arrange for a secular funeral. One family chose to read the story of Mr Happy as it was their son's favourite. Another family chose the Snowman song, and another chose to have the song *Bright Eyes*. Each family should be able to plan, with the help of the clergy, or whoever will be taking the funeral, the contents and style which suits that family. Some choose to have a service full of praise and thanksgiving for the life that is ended, inviting family and friends to join them. Others have a very quiet service on their own. Some families decide to have no flowers, others have many. It may be helpful to make a tape recording of the service, to share with people who may not be able to attend. And because many families are too distressed to take in the details of the service, a tape can be listened to later, at a more peaceful time. Other families like to have service sheets printed. This need not cost a great deal of money, and the service sheets can be sent to those who could not go to the funeral, as well as kept by those who do.

Once the funeral is over, then the long hard days of bereavement begin. For the first few weeks after the funeral there are usually plenty of people around, as friends and family keep in touch, but gradually, as others begin to get on with their own lives, the bereaved may start to feel very alone. It is after those first few weeks, when the numbness and shock gradually fade and the reality of what has happened begins to strike home, that other people start to move away. It seems that just at the moment when other people are most needed, they start to disappear.

It is not easy to help newly bereaved people. Often they will refuse offers of help, but at the same time will say that no one is coming near them. Perhaps the most important rule to follow is that just because someone has said "No" once to offers of help, it does not necessarily follow that they will feel the same way a few weeks later. A friend or relative should not be deterred by an initial rejection, often made during a period of numbness and shock. Sometimes the bereaved will be moody and difficult; at other times they may seem fine. Whatever their mood, bereaved parents always need a chance to say how they are *really* feeling. Families often say that when people ask: "How are you?" it does not seem to be a real question; it can appear that the questioner does not really want to hear the answer. As a result, an "I'm fine" is tossed off, an answer which conceals the fact that inside there is turmoil and distress. A well made-up face may be like a mask hiding something. When someone says "I'm fine" too glibly, it may be the right moment just to ask quietly: "Is that the whole truth? How are you *really*?" Showing that you genuinely want to know can open a door and the true feelings will be spoken about, often with tremendous relief. A mask needs to slip if the sufferer is to find the comfort and support which can be given by a genuinely caring person.

One of the biggest problems which can occur in a bereaved family is that different people grieve in different ways, and these differences often lead to many misunderstandings. Mothers may say: "My husband doesn't cry any more; I don't think he cares any longer that his child has died." Fathers may say: "My wife thinks that I don't care because I don't cry. She doesn't know that every day on the way home from work, I stop and have a cry on my own. I don't like crying with other people." Too easily, we think that we are good at "knowing" how others should behave. We should take more care to let them react in their own ways, and to make no judgement.

When two people are grieving deeply, it can be very difficult for them to be able to help each other. Often it is at the very time when a partner's help is most needed that it may not be forthcoming, because they are each struggling to help themselves, and have no energy to help each other. A common dilemma is that fathers often grieve much later than mothers. It seems that fathers have to get on with life, have to go back to work, and possibly try to support a very broken wife. They may shelve their personal grieving until their partner has started to recover. Encouragement may be needed to enable parents to look at such delayed grief, and recognise it for what it is.

It can be argued that fathers have a particularly hard time when their child dies. The ever-present image that men should keep a "stiff upper lip" makes it extremely difficult for them to grieve openly. In addition, people often make the assumption that it is only the mother who really grieves. One father told me about the many people who had come up to him and said: "I was so sorry to hear about your daughter. How is your wife?" He wanted to reply: "She was *my* daughter as well as my wife's." It was painful to him when the assumption was made that because he was a man he did not feel as upset as his wife did.

In the same way that parents may have come to resent aspects of each other's pattern of life before the death of their child, so after the death, the same thing may occur. The mother may resent the father going out to work, and not appearing to have lost the routine and pattern of life. The father, in turn, may long to have the opportunity to sit at home, as his wife can, hidden from the outside world, and grieving without the pressure of having to continue working and facing people every day.

If a child has been ill over a period of months or years, the mother will almost always have been the chief carer. She will have become a considerable expert in that field, and will probably have had to drop many other activities in order to give constant care to her sick child. Many things may have suffered because of this, especially her relationships with the rest of the family. Once the child has died, the mother's main role as carer has gone. What gave her recognition and confidence, and may have fed her love and given her a purpose, has gone. This can be an exceptionally difficult time for the woman. She may find that she has grown apart from her husband, and that they need to work at getting to know each other again. The rest of the family may have become used to looking after themselves, and resent their mother trying to take over their lives again.

There are many hurdles for a family to overcome, events which cause great emotional difficulties. These may be financial: for example, all the allowances that they received for the sick child will be stopped. Attendance allowance, mobility allowance (which may have been financing a car) and family allowance will all cease quite abruptly. The family is free now to go shopping at any time, no longer tied down by a sick child, but at this very point the sudden financial change may make such family shopping expeditions impossible because money is much tighter.

But there are other hurdles as well. There may have been many people calling at the house to help with the child's care. After the child's death they will probably stop calling, and so the parents feel very isolated. They may be continually affected emotionally by ordinary events in their everyday life, such as seeing other children going to school. Automatically laying a place at the table for the dead child may cause sudden and deep distress. It can be difficult to answer people who ask: "How many children have you got?" Should the dead child be included? But then it has to be explained that one child has died. If the child who has died is excluded, then there may be strong feelings of guilt at having left them out. Many mothers say that weekends are difficult because the family should all be together. Others may find that the weekdays drag by and that they prefer the weekend because more members of the family are around.

Going shopping and seeing endless things that the dead child would have liked can also be difficult. Some mothers continue to buy things for their child, even though the child has died. The very fact of buying something, even if the child is dead, can be difficult to stop, because to stop means facing the reality of the child's death. Mothers who do this shopping need very gentle help in order to understand that such behaviour is unrealistic. Sometimes there may be a fear of others knowing about such behaviour patterns and a friend may be asked: "Please don't tell anyone; I must be going mad." Often all that is needed is reassurance that they are not alone and that other mothers have behaved in the same way without being considered mad. It is not uncommon to buy something for all the family, including the dead child, and to forget that there is one fewer than there was. A mother bought things for her children's Christmas stockings. When she got to the checkout she realised that she had bought something for the dead child. She said later: "I felt like throwing them all on the floor and running out of the shop." How helpful it is to have a caring friend to talk to at times like this.

Any gathering, especially when all the family are together, can leave an obviously empty place at the table. The other children in the family may say things that are difficult for their parents to accept calmly. For example: "I wish I was not an only child", or "I want my brother back", or again "I want someone to play with", or "Anyone would think that my sister was a saint with all the fuss that everyone is making – she wasn't so wonderful", or, a last example, "Why can't we be happy again?" Parents have to accept that these seemingly aggressive statements are part of the child's own grieving pattern and bewilderment, and that children, too, must work out their pain in their own way.

Many parents will say that life loses its meaning, and that there is no purpose to anything. The things in life which used to seem important, like buying the latest car or acquiring material possessions, take on a completely different meaning, and come to seem quite unimportant. To those whose child has died, other people's hard luck stories can seem irritating and petty. How can they feel distressed over such everyday events as a car breaking down or a child having a cold? Those who have been bereaved will say that nothing worse than the death of their child could ever happen to them, and so nothing in anyone else's experience seems important. Bereaved people also often suffer from great lethargy, and even the smallest tasks seem to require a huge effort.

Christmas can be a very hard time for all the family, especially if there are other children. It is a time when everyone is meant to be happy when the last thing the family may feel like is being happy. Many families go away for Christmas in order to break the pattern of the previous years. It can be very difficult for the family to know just what to write in a Christmas card. If the dead child is left out, that can feel wrong. However to include the child may also feel wrong. Sometimes the easiest way can be to write: *From all the Smiths*. In that way, the dead child is included without the trauma of having to say anything explicit. Similarly, when sending a Christmas card to a bereaved family, one can write: *To the Smith family*. In that way the family then feels that their dead child is included as well. One family, when receiving a pile of presents at Christmas, also received some flowers to go on their daughter's grave. They said that it was a comfort to think that someone had remembered her at that time. Gestures like this can make a great difference.

The time spent visiting a child's grave will vary from family to family. Some families gain strength from tending the grave and keeping it looking beautiful with flowers and plants, while others find no comfort at all from such activities. Choosing a headstone usually happens some months after the funeral. Many families have said how painful it was to see the headstone in place for the first time. Seeing the child's name and date of death engraved in stone brings home once more the reality of the death.

The remaining children in the family may find life very hard. Living with grieving parents is not easy for a child. Sometimes children can be quite severely neglected by parents wrapped up in their own grief and finding it hard to help the remaining children. Bereaved parents are often listless, and can be snappy or easily roused to anger. Little things irritate them, and make them impatient. For children to understand their parents' behaviour at such a time is very difficult. To see his parents crying may be distressing to a child, and can cause him to wonder whether they would have preferred it if he had died rather than his brother or sister, since everything that he does seems to irritate his father or mother.

Parents should try to avoid putting the dead child on a pedestal. If they do so, the remaining children may find it very hard to live up to the saintly image that is constantly before them. It is unfair to other children, possibly still grieving themselves, to make comparisons with the child who has died. The bewilderment such behaviour can arouse may be helped if children have someone they can trust to turn to for additional support at this time, and to whom they can talk if things at home are difficult. It may be that a teacher at school can help. Certainly the child's teacher should be very aware of what is going on at home, not just during the immediate aftermath of the death, but also to be aware that the grieving may go on for some years. Very many families say that the second year after a child dies is harder than the first. If a teacher is not aware of this, she may not understand why a bereaved child is behaving in a certain way. Being alert to these children, and understanding how they are feeling, can make a big difference. Where a child has moved to a new school after the death of a brother or sister, the new school should be told of the death in case a delayed reaction occurs. A caring adult outside the family can play an enormously important role in a child's life after a bereavement.

When a child reaches the same age as the brother or sister was when he or she died, problems can arise. The child may feel guilty at having lived longer, or afraid that he may die because a brother or sister died at this age. This is another point at which it can be valuable for the child to have an older friend to talk to about these feelings.

When a family decides that the time has come to clear up their dead child's bedroom, it can be helpful if their other children are present. It is then possible to say openly to them something like: "These things are now yours. I am sure your brother would have liked you to have them." This is always a very hard thing to do, because it is saying to all the family: "He is dead and no longer needs these things." Families often find clearing up the room very hard. It is important that there should be no hurry to do this, but equally it is important that it should eventually happen. This is because it is a recognition of the reality that the dead child no longer needs his possessions. It is often a painful thing to do, but grieving is all about the process of letting go. When anyone dies, the bereaved need through their grieving to "let go" of the dead person. This is not to forget them, but to stop living in the shadow of their death. It could be said that someone has "let go" when they feel that they can get on with their own life again.

There are certain physical reactions which some people feel after a bereavement. No one person will react in the same way, but many people find that they have similar reactions. One of the most helpful things that a visitor can do is to give reassurance that there is nothing wrong or unusual about the way the bereaved are feeling. Most mothers will say at some time: "I feel as if I am going mad" or "I hurt so much that I am not sure that I can go on much longer", "My arms feel so empty". Some physical feelings can be frightening: people speak of feeling sick, of wanting to swallow all the time, feeling pregnant, or of feeling as if they are choking. These are all common reactions, but very distressing to the sufferer. It is a time when the support and understanding of friends who are prepared just to *listen* and give reassurance is very important indeed. Friends should be prepared to sit with the bereaved, and just let them talk.

It is common for the bereaved to feel great anger, and this may be directed at anyone or anything. Mothers feel anger at the apparent insensitivity of other women, who seem to do nothing but talk about their own children or schools or clothes or toys. Everywhere they go there seem to be happy mothers and children. Sometimes they see mothers getting cross with their children, and may be tempted to tell them how grateful they should be to have a child at all. Parents who long for another child seem to see pregnant women all the time, which can fill them with a painful anger and resentment.

Anger can fasten on to anyone who is at hand. Sometimes it is directed at people in the family; sometimes strangers, or even at what is being said on television. Often it will be directed at God or the representatives of the Church; doctors or nurses may also be a source of anger. Even the child who has died may sometimes be angrily attacked: "How dare he leave me?" Such comprehensive anger can be very frightening for all concerned, including the bereaved person expressing the anger. Again, it is important for friends, who may be taken aback by the vehemence of the anger, *not* to be frightened away, or to take it personally. The strength of a friend's capacity to understand what lies behind the anger is of vital importance, as is the continuance of loving support.

Sometimes very unhelpful remarks are made: "You can always have another child", as if that would replace the dead child. Another baby might be what the parents want, but it would *not* be a replacement. When there are other children in the family, people may even say: "Aren't you blessed to have other children." Bereaved parents may draw comfort from having other children, but they will still feel the loss of their dead child, and such remarks are inappropriate. It is also not very helpful to say, "You'll get over it in time." The immediate pains of grief do lessen in time, but the experience of the death remains, and is not erased.

Some people experience "visions" of their dead child. They may either have a strong feeling of presence in the room with them, or of actually seeing the child. This can happen either at night in a dark room or in full daylight. It is not known exactly what happens on such occasions, but it is quite clear that the experience can be a very real one. Sometimes it will feel good, and sometimes very frightening. If it has been frightening, reassurance may be needed. Often people have very vivid dreams of their child and will wake expecting to find them alive and well again. Such dreams can cause more heartache, or they can bring a feeling of peace. There is no "norm".

One of the greatest sources of distress to a parent can be the feeling of not being able to sense any longer what the dead child looked, felt, smelled, or even sounded like. Some families will have video film of the child which may eventually bring great comfort, but it can also be distressing to see the video too soon after the death.

Many people find that they go through a period of searching for their child, feeling a strong need to find out where he is and if all is well. This can lead to visits to a spiritualist. My own experience is that on the whole families have not found this produces a long-term answer. They may explore this road for a while, but eventually realise that it will not bring back the dead child.

It can sometimes be particularly difficult for those parents who believe in life after death. It is often assumed that because of their belief they will not, or should not, grieve. Of course a faith in a life after death can bring peace and hope, but it does not diminish the sense of loss nor the physical processes of grieving. For Christians, the Bible offers many examples of people grieving after the death of a loved one, notably Jesus weeping after the death of Lazarus.

These are only a few examples of the many and varied experiences that can befall bereaved families. Not everyone will experience the same feelings, but many are common to bereaved families.

What marks the end of bereavement? Does it ever go away? I am sure that no family is ever the same after a child has died, and I suspect that no family would wish to be the same. Suffering a deep and painful bereavement does change people. Some will say that they have grown through the experience. Others feel destroyed by it, and seem never to "get over it". I think that most would say that there will always be a small part of them that remains sad. One mother said, four years after her daughter died, "I can now remember her without the stabbing pain. There is still sadness, but it isn't a painful sadness." Another woman talked with tears in her eyes of her son who had died ten years earlier. She said: "I am happy now, but there will always be a little bit of me that is sad."

It is very important to remember that grief does not go away quickly. Most families say that the second year is worse than the first. This may be because it is difficult to go on pretending that the child is on a long holiday and then the reality and the finality of death starts to strike home. By the fourth year, life is often returning to some normality again; to a new and readjusted pattern.

Occasionally it may happen that parents suffer a reaction to the death of their child many years afterwards. It is important for others to accept this and give reassurance that such grieving is permissible, even after such a long time.

I have tried in this book to share with others what the many families I visit have told me. No one family copes with bereavement in the same way, but there are many similar experiences that bereaved families share.

Being so close to the death of children makes one aware how fragile life is, what a precious gift it is, and that it should not be taken for granted. I have been given that awareness by the families I have been privileged to know, and I thank them for letting me walk the road with them for a little while.

PART TWO

MY BROTHER

A STORY FOR CHILDREN

My brother is very ill – not just ill like having a cold or mumps, but really ill, so that he cannot often play with me. And he seems to sleep a lot. I wish he was well.

Sometimes he goes to hospital, and I stay at home with Dad, because Mum goes to hospital with my brother. And sometimes, when my brother is really bad, Dad and Mum both go to the hospital and I stay with friends. I miss us all being at home together.

One night Mum and Dad came into my bedroom and talked to me about my brother. They said the doctors told them he wouldn't live much longer and that he was dying. I felt frightened and sad.

But my brother has come home again. He has a bed in the sitting-room. He doesn't do much. Sometimes he smiles, but a lot of the time he is grumpy, even when people come to see him and bring him presents. Sometimes they bring things for me, but not often.

I wish our home could be the way it used to be. Now there are so many people coming in and out – nurses and doctors and friends. Mum often seems tired and cross. She and Dad keep going out of the room and talking quietly to each other. I wish they would talk to me. My brother seems to sleep all the time now. His breathing is funny. Mum says she thinks he will die soon. I asked her what would happen when he died. She said he would stop breathing and that his heart would stop beating. Then he would go very cold.

Early one morning, Mum came in and woke me up. She hugged me very hard and said my brother was dead. She took me in to see him, and he wasn't breathing. He was still and cold. He looked like my brother, but different, as if something was missing.

I helped Mum and Dad to wash him and dress him in his favourite track suit, the one he liked best of all. We cried, all together, and I felt so sad. I wish my brother was still alive.

Later in the morning, some men came and put my brother in a coffin. My mum said the men were undertakers, and that they would get everything ready for my brother's funeral. The coffin was like a large box with a white lining; my brother looked quite comfortable in it. We put his teddy bear in with him, and then the undertakers put a lid on the coffin and took it away.

Lots of friends and people from our church came to see us. We talked about the funeral and chose some hymns and songs to sing. I chose one I know my brother liked. I asked where my brother was now, and Mum said he was in a peaceful place which is sometimes called Heaven. I said, "But his body was in that coffin." Then Mum said that the special part of him, the part which made him who he was, his soul, had flown from his body, like a butterfly freeing itself from a chrysalis. Now my brother is free from all pain, and he isn't ill any more. I hope he is happy.

Later we all went to my brother's funeral. My uncles and aunts and my cousins and lots of my brother's friends were there, and there were flowers everywhere. I didn't like it when the coffin was taken away. I felt sad and lonely, and I held Mum's hand. Everyone was crying, even Dad and Grandad. Now I don't have a brother to play with any more, and I will miss him so much.

After the funeral, everyone came to our house for a cup of tea. It was like a party, but a sad party. My brother would have liked to be with us. It is strange without him.

Today we sorted out my brother's things. Mum and Dad said I could have some of his toys, so I chose lots of them, and put them away in my bedroom. Mum said she knew my brother would want me to have them.

I stayed away from school for a little while and when I went back my friends were glad to see me. But when I come home from school and my brother is not there, I feel sad. Then Mum and I talk about him, and tell each other how much we miss him.

Sometimes we go and put flowers on his grave, and we think of all the happy times we had. Mum cries a lot, and says she hurts inside she misses my brother so much. It frightens me when she cries, but she seems to cheer up again afterwards. Dad is sad too, and sometimes we are all sad together. We try to help each other through the sad times.

My family will never be the same without my brother. We are slowly getting used to him not being there. We are not forgetting him, just learning to live without him. My friends at school don't talk about my brother much now.

They think it will make me sad, but I wish they *would* talk about him. I want his name to be part of my life now, even if he isn't around any more. He was my brother, and I will never forget him.

PRAYERS, POEMS & READINGS

Death is nothing at all . . . I have only slipped away into the next room. I am I, and you are you. Whatever we were to each other, that we are still. Call me by my old familiar name. Speak to me in the easy way which you always used. Put no differences into your tone. Wear no forced air of solemnity or sorrow. Laugh as we always laughed at the little jokes we enjoyed together. Play, smile, think of me. Let my name be ever the household name that it always was. Let it be spoken without effort, without the ghost of a shadow on it. Life means all that it ever meant. It is the same as it ever was. There is absolutely unbroken continuity. What is this death but a negligible accident? Why should I be out of mind because I am out of sight? I am waiting for you for an interval somewhere very near . . . just round the corner. All is well.

Canon Scott Holland

Then Aslan turned to them and said:

"You do not yet look so happy as I mean you to be."

Lucy said, "We're so afraid of being sent away again, Aslan. And you have sent us back into our world so often."

"No fear of that," said Aslan. "Have you not guessed?"

Their hearts leaped and a wild hope rose within them.

"There was a real railway accident," said Aslan softly. "Your father and mother and all of you are, as you used to call it, in the Shadowland, dead. The term is over: the holidays have begun. The dream is ended: this is the morning."

And as He spoke He no longer looked to them like a lion; but the things that began to happen after that were so great and beautiful that I cannot write them. And for us this is the end of all the stories, and we can most truly say that all lived happily ever after. But for them it was only the beginning of the real story. All their life in the world and all their adventures in Narnia had only been the cover and the title page:

now at last they were beginning Chapter One of The Great Story which no one on earth has read; which goes on for ever; in which every chapter is better than the one before.

C.S. Lewis, from *The Last Battle*

They all felt awkward and unhappy suddenly because it was a sort of goodbye they were saying, and they didn't want to think about it.
Then Christopher Robin called out, "Pooh!"
"Yes," said Pooh.
"When I'm . . . when . . . Pooh!"
"Yes, Christopher Robin?"
"I'm not going to do nothing any more."
"Never again?"
"Well, not so much. They don't let you."
Pooh waited for him to go on, but he was silent again.
"Yes, Christopher Robin?" said Pooh helpfully.
"Pooh, when I'm . . . you know, when I'm not doing Nothing, will you come up here sometimes?"
"Just me?"
"Yes, Pooh."
"Will you be here too?"
"Yes Pooh, I will be really, I promise I will be, Pooh."
"That's good," said Pooh.
"Pooh, promise you won't forget about me, ever. Not even when I'm a hundred."
"I promise," he said.
"Pooh, whatever happens, you will understand, won't you?"

A.A. Milne, from *The House At Pooh Corner*

He said to them, "Let the children come to me; do not try to stop them; for the kingdom of God belongs to such as these. I tell you, whoever does not accept the kingdom of God like a child, will never enter it." And he put his arms round them, laid his hands upon them and blessed them.

Mark 10: verses 14–17 (*The New English Bible*)

At that time the disciples came to Jesus and asked, "Who is the greatest in the kingdom of Heaven?" He called a child, set him in front of them, and said, "I tell you this: unless you turn round and become like children, you will never enter the kingdom of Heaven. Let a man humble himself till he is like this child, and he will be the greatest in the kingdom of Heaven.

"Never despise one of these little ones; I tell you, they have their guardian angels in Heaven, who look continually on the face of my heavenly Father."

Matthew 18: verses 1–5 and 10 (*The New English Bible*)

With this in mind, then, I kneel in prayer to the Father,
from whom every family in heaven and on earth takes its name,
that out of the treasures in his glory he may grant you strength and power through His Spirit in your inner being,
that through faith, Christ may dwell in your hearts in love.
With deep roots and firm foundations, may you be strong to grasp, with all God's people, what is the breadth and length and height and depth of the love of Christ, and to know it, though it is beyond knowledge.
So you may attain to fullness of being, the fullness of God himself.

Ephesians 3: verses 14–19 (*The New English Bible*)

Set your troubled hearts at rest.
Trust in God always; trust also in me.
There are many dwelling places in my Father's house;
if it were not so I should have told you;
For I am going there on purpose to prepare a place for you.
And if I go and prepare a place for you,
I shall come again and receive you to myself,
so that where I am you may be also;
and my way there is known to you.

John 14: verses 1–4 (*The New English Bible*)

For no one of us lives, and equally no one of us dies, for himself alone.
If we live, we live for the Lord; and if we die, we die for the Lord.
Whether therefore we live or die, we belong to the Lord.

Romans 14: verses 7–9 (*The New English Bible*)

My beloved answered, he said to me;
"Rise up, my darling;
my fairest, come away.
For now the winter is past,
the rains are over and gone;
the flowers appear in the country-side;
the time is coming when the birds will sing,
and the turtle-dove's cooing will be heard in our land;
when the green figs will ripen on the fig trees
and the vines give forth their fragrance.
Rise up, my darling;
my fairest, come away."

Song of Songs 2: verses 10–13 (*The New English Bible*)

I am standing on the sea shore. A ship sails and spreads her white sails to the morning breeze and starts for the ocean. She is an object of beauty and I stand watching her till at last she fades on the horizon, and someone at my side says, "She is gone." Gone where? Gone from my sight, that is all; she is just as large in the masts, hull and spars as she was when I saw her, and just as able to bear her load of living freight to its destination.

The diminished size and total loss of sight is in me, not in her; and just at the moment when someone at my side says, "She is gone", there are others who are watching her coming, and other voices take up a glad shout, "There she comes", and that is DYING.

Bishop Brent

The Bright Field

I have seen the sun break through
to illuminate a small field
for a while, and gone my way
and forgotten it. But that was the pearl
of great price, the one field that had treasure in it.
I realise now that I must give all that I have
to possess it. Life is not hurrying
on to a receding future, nor hankering after
an imagined past. It is turning
aside like Moses to see the miracle
of the lit bush, to a brightness
that seemed as transitory as your youth
once, but is the eternity that awaits you.

R.S. Thomas

He whom we love and lose is no longer where he was before; he is now wherever we are.

St John Chrysostom

. . . the deceased has removed into a better country, and bounded away to a happier inheritance; . . . thou hast not lost thy son, but bestowed him henceforth in an inviolable spot. Say not then, I pray thee, I am no longer called 'father', for why art thou no longer called so, when thy son abideth? For surely thou didst not part with thy child, nor lose thy son? Rather thou hast gotten him, and hast him in greater safety. Wherefore, no longer shalt thou be called 'father' here only, but also in heaven; so that thou hast not lost the title 'father' here only, but hast gained it in a nobler sense; for henceforth thou shalt be called father not of a mortal child, but of an immortal . . . For think not, because he is not present, that therefore he is lost; for had he been absent in a foreign land, the title of thy relationship had not gone from thee with his body.

Source unknown

And a woman who held a babe against her bosom said, "Speak to us of Children."
And he said: "Your children are not your children,
They are the sons and daughters of Life's longing for itself.
They come through you but not from you,
And though they are with you,
Yet they belong not to you.

You may give them your love but not your thoughts,
For they have their own thoughts.
You may house their bodies but not their souls,
For their souls dwell in the house of tomorrow,
Which you cannot visit, not even in your dreams.
You may strive to be like them, but seek not to make them like you.
For life goes not backward nor tarries with yesterday.

You are the bows from which your children as living arrows are sent forth.
The Archer sees the mark upon the path of the infinite, and He bends you with all His might, that His arrow may go swift and far.
Let your bending in the Archer's hand be for gladness;
For even as He loves the arrow that flies,
So He loves also the bow that is stable.

Then a woman said, Speak to us of Joy and Sorrow.
And he answered:
Your joy is your sorrow unmasked.
And the selfsame well from which your laughter rises was oftentimes filled with your tears.
And how else can it be?
The deeper that sorrow carves into your being, the more joy you can contain.
Is not the cup that holds your wine the very cup that was burned in the potter's oven?
And is not the lute that soothes your spirit the very wood that was hollowed by knives?

When you are joyous, look deep into your heart and you shall find it is only that which has given you sorrow that is giving you joy.

Kahlil Gibran, from *The Prophet*

If I should die and leave you here awhile,
Be not like others, sore undone, who keep
Long vigils by the silent dust, and weep.
For my sake, turn again to life and smile,
Nerving thy heart and trembling hand to do
Something to comfort weaker hearts than thine,
Complete those dear unfinished tasks of mine,
And I perchance may therein comfort you.

A. Price Hughes

Welcoming a special child

A meeting was held quite far from earth;
It's time again for another birth.
Said the angels to the Lord above,
"This special child will need much love.

He may not run or laugh or play;
His thoughts may seem quite far away.
In many ways he won't adapt,
And he'll be known as handicapped.

So let's be careful where he's sent;
We want his life to be content.
Please, Lord, find parents who
Will do a special job for you.

They will not realise right away
The leading role they're asked to play;
But with this child sent from above
Comes stronger faith and richer love.

And soon they'll know the privilege given
In caring for their gift from heaven;
Their precious charge, so meek and mild,
Is heaven's very special child."

Edna Massimilla

We let them return to Thee, who gave them to us;
And as Thou didst not lose them in giving, so we have not lost them in returning.
Life is eternal, and love is immortal, and death is only an horizon, and an horizon is nothing save the limits of our sight.
Lift us up, O strong Son of God, that we may see further.
Open our eyes that we may see more clearly.

Source unknown

I said to the man who stood at the Gate of the Year, "Give me a light that I may tread safely into the unknown." And he replied, "Go out into the darkness and put your hand into the hand of God. That shall be to you better than light and safer than a known way."

Minnie Haskyns

I had thought that your death
Was a waste and a destruction,
A pain of grief hardly to be endured.
I am only beginning to learn
That your life was a gift and a growing
And a loving left with me.
The desperation of death
Destroyed the existence of love,
But the fact of death
Cannot destroy what has been given.
I am learning to look at life again
Instead of your death and your departing.

Marjorie Pizer, *The Existence of Love*

If I should go before the rest of you
Break not a flower nor inscribe a stone,
Nor when I'm gone speak in a Sunday voice
But be the usual selves that I have known,
Weep if you must,
Parting is hell,
But life goes on
So sing as well.

Joyce Grenfell

Mary Poppins had gone. Jane read the note she had left.
"Mrs. Brill!" she called. "What does 'Au Revoir' mean?"
"I think, Miss Jane dear, it means 'To meet again'."
Jane and Michael looked at each other. Joy and understanding shone in their eyes. They knew what Mary Poppins meant.
Michael gave a long sigh of relief. "That's all right," he said shakily. "She always does what she says she will."
He turned away.
"Michael, are you crying?" Jane asked.
He twisted his head and tried to smile at her,
"No, I'm not," he said. "It is only my eyes."

P. L. Travers, from *Mary Poppins*

Roads go ever ever on
Over rock and under tree,
By caves where never sun has shone,
By streams that never find the sea.
Over snow by winter sown,
And through the merry flowers of June,
Over grass and over stone,
And under mountains in the moon.

Roads go ever ever on
Under clouds and under stars,
Yet feet that wandering have gone
Turn at last to home afar.
Eyes that fire and sword have seen
And horror in the halls of stone,
Look at last on meadows green,
And trees and hills they long have known.

J.R.R. Tolkien, from *The Hobbit*

May the road rise to meet you.
May the wind be always at your back.
May the sun shine warm upon your face.
May the rain fall softly upon your fields until we meet again.
May God hold you in the hollow of His hand.

Doris Stickney, *Old Gaelic Blessing*

I was a little stranger, which, at my entrance into the world, was saluted and surrounded with innumerable joys. My knowledge was divine . . . My very ignorance was advantageous. I seemed as one brought into the Estate of Innocence. All things were spotless and pure and glorious: yea, and infinitely mine, and joyful and precious. I knew not that there were any sins or complaints or laws. I dreamed not of poverties, contentions or vices. All tears and quarrels were hidden from my eyes. Everything was at rest, free and immortal. I knew nothing of sickness or death or rents or exaction, either for tribute or bread. In the absence of these I entertained like an angel with the work of God in their splendour and glory, I saw all in the peace of Eden; heaven and earth did sing my Creator's praises, and could not make more melody to Adam than to me. All time was eternity and a perpetual Sabbath. Is it not strange that an infant should be heir of the whole world, and see those mysteries which the books of the learned never unfold?

Thomas Traherne

They are not lost, our dearest loves,
Nor have they travelled far,
Just stepped inside home's loveliest room,
And left the door ajar . . .

Source unknown

We cannot judge a biography by its length, by the number of pages in it: we must judge by the richness of the contents . . . Sometimes the 'unfinisheds' are among the most beautiful symphonies.

Viktor Frankl

I have seen death too often to believe in death.
It is not an ending, but a withdrawal.
As one who finishes a long journey,
Stills the motor,
Turns off the lights,
Steps from the car,
And walks up the path
To the home that awaits him.

Source unknown

Love is this
That you lived amongst us these few years
And taught us love.

Love is this
That you died amongst us and helped us
To the source of life.

With all our love
We wish you bon voyage.

Love lives.

Lindy Hemmy

. . . I imagined I had lived in the time of Christ. How lucky that would have been, I thought . . .
And then it struck me and was so real. Christ does live, and we *do* live in the same time. No wishing and no 'if onlys'. Christ does live and his Love is here. He alone has never moved. That is the statement of the Resurrection. Nothing dies and nothing ends. When we reach one conclusion we only become part of another beginning. Your father wrote it in his Gardening Log; "*Every seed has its Easter*". Now finally, I understand.

Paula d'Arcy

I dreamt that the time had come to carry back to my Father
The treasures I was sent to gather on earth.
So I held out my chalice to my brother angel to be filled with the values of my life.
I thought of bright achievement, of renown and success,
but they vanished in the emptiness of glamour.
When it was handed back to me,
I found my cup filled to the brim with what I thought were tiny things,
hardly noticed and long forgotten,
but now, sparkling with the inner light of the love they contained.
Then I walked holding high the grail of my soul
and there was joy in heaven.

Fernand de Vinck

ADDRESSES OF SUPPORT GROUPS

Cruse, Cruse House, 126 Sheen Road, Richmond, Surrey TW9 1UR 081 940 4818 *Bereavement care*

ACT, Institute of Child Health, Royal Hospital for Sick Children, St Michael's Hill, Bristol BS2 8BJ 0272 221556 *Action for the care of families whose children have life-threatening and terminal conditions*

Compassionate Friends, 6 Denmark Street, Bristol BS1 5DQ 0272 292778 *Bereaved parents offer friendship and understanding to other bereaved parents*

Parents of Murdered Children Support Group, 10 Eastern Avenue, Prittlewell, Southend on Sea, Essex SS2 5QU 0702 68510 *Part of Compassionate Friends*

The Foundation for the Study of Infant Deaths, 15 Belgrave Square, London SW1X 8PS 071 235 1721 and 071 235 0965 *Offers help and support to parents whose children have died from 'Cot Deaths'. Also funds research into the causes of 'Cot Deaths'*

Twins and Multiple Births Association (TAMBA), TAMBA Secretary, 59 Sunnyside, Worksop, North Notts. F81 FLN 0909 47925 *Bereavement support group*

The Lisa Sainsbury Foundation, 8-10 Crown Hill, Croydon, Surrey CR0 1RY 081 686 8808 *Supports staff working with the dying*

SANDS, 28 Portland Place, London W1N 4DE 071 436 5881 *Stillbirth and Neonatal Deaths*

CHILDREN'S HOSPICES *These offer respite care and terminal care to children with life-threatening illnesses*

HELEN HOUSE, 37 Leopold Street, Oxford OX4 1QT 0865 728251

MARTIN HOUSE, Grove Road, Clifford, Wetherby, West Yorkshire LS23 6TX 0937 845045

ACORNS, 103 Oak Tree Lane, Selly Oak, Birmingham B29 6HZ 021 414 1741

CAMBRIDGE CHILDREN'S HOSPICE, The Old Rectory, Milton, Cambridge CB4 4AB 022 386 0306

ACKNOWLEDGEMENTS

The Author and Publisher are indebted to the following for the use of copyright material: Fernand de Vinck; Lion Publishing Plc and Harold Shaw Publishers, USA, for *A Song For Sarah* by Paula d'Arcy; Hodder and Stoughton for the extract by Viktor Frankl from *Man's Search for Meaning*; Methuen London for the extract from *The House at Pooh Corner* by A.A. Milne; Heinemann Ltd for the extracts from *The Prophet* by Kahlil Gibran; Second Back Row Press, Australia, and Marjorie Pizer for the poem *The Existence of Love* from *To You, the Living*; Richard Scott Simon Ltd for "If I should go . . ." by Joyce Grenfell © The Joyce Grenfell Memorial Trust 1980; Macmillan London Ltd for *The Bright Field* by R.S. Thomas from *Later Poems*; Collins Publishers for the extract from *Mary Poppins* by P.L. Travers; Collins Publishers for the extract from *The Last Battle* by C.S. Lewis; Allen & Unwin for the extract from *The Hobbit* by J.R.R. Tolkien; Darton, Longman and Todd for "Death is nothing at all . . ." by Canon Scott Holland from *All at the Harvest End*. The passages from the Bible have been taken from *The New English Bible*, Second Edition © 1970 By permission of Oxford and Cambridge University Presses.

In some cases it has proved impossible to locate sources of quotations included, although every effort has been made. If, however, any query should arise it should be addressed to the Publisher.